YEAR OF THE WASP

Joel Deane is the author of *The Norseman's Song;
Another; Catch and Kill: the Politics of Power;* and two
collections of poetry, *Magisterium* and *Subterranean
Radio Songs.* He has been a finalist for the Walkley
Award and the Melbourne Prize for Literature, and
been shortlisted for the Anne Elder Award.

Hunter Contemporary Australian Poets

YEAR OF
THE WASP

JOEL DEANE

*For Andy / Sorry to miss
you in Belfast.*

H
HUNTER

Joel Deane

Hunter Publishers
PO Box 6077
Santa Lucia
Queensland, 4067
Australia
www.hunterpublishers.com.au

Hunter Contemporary Australian Poets
Series Editor: Jessica Wilkinson

Cover design: Design by Committee

Cover image: adapted from Meredith Squires, Mountain. City.
From the series 'Eight Views of Nowhere', 2013.
Archival digital print, five panels, each 40 cm x 151 cm.
Copyright © Meredith Squires

National Library of Australia
Cataloguing-in-Publication data:

Deane, Joel
Year of the Wasp
ISBN: 9780994352859 (pbk.)
Hunter Contemporary Australian Poets ; 11

For my second wife.

❦ Contents ❦

YEAR OF THE WASP

South of Shepp,
the Renault punched a hole
        the shape of the first man
in a storm of locusts.
Confirming the irrigation flats
as God's chosen wasteland.
        At the Base Hospital,
the old man was sleeping,
hooked up like a cow
in the shed for milking.
The son domed the cap
        of his father's freckled skull
with the cup of the palm of his hand;
watched him breathe
            like a toothless babe.
The air conditioning was far too cold.

It was foolish to hope. He prayed
for rain but the heavens let fall
Tithonus instead,
whose every atom
was transfigured into a wasp. And
every wasp was born in fury
and showered down and
stung and did not slake the thirst.
Made unbelievers believe: lured
the fervent into car parks
seeking rapture, where the wasps
and not the Lord were waiting.
And the supplicant —
whose waking prayer invited wrath
— did not run. Did not dare.
Neither fervent nor fallen,
he knew better than to quit
kneeling in his suburban driveway.
Knew safety to be mythology:
a place sustained by misplaced belief.
Stayed put instead,
eyes closed, like a child
counting down from
ten to one before
it is time to seek.

Paramedics arrive.
Give him a shot of Stemetil
          as he thinks of holding
a match burning down
to the pinch, of a summer sun setting
behind a line of Norfolk pines,
of the resonance of cicadas in January,
of men loading fishing boats onto
                    weeping trailers —
He murmurs as they cart him from the house,
'Love is like the pilot of a TV series never made.
          Not enough.'
He slurs, 'I have to spew.'
And the ambo goes,
'Use the bag, champ.'
And the nurse goes,
'Do you know where you are?'
And he goes,
'In an ambulance.'
Although he isn't. Not anymore.
          And the interrogations begin as
stalactites of blood
                    coagulate, sharpen
into stakes above bed eight.

The giant toad squatting,
dead centre of the room,
is not a figment,
but a fact. He lies on
its white tongue as a black swan
of a woman wheels above him.

Feathers tickle skin that covers
the too-small skull that is his face;
remind him of Coole,
of a funeral
in his brain, of nothing.
Smiling, she says, 'So,

you want Miles Davis.' Shows
a set of small white baby teeth
that were never lost, slides
the tongue back inside
the gullet, where he lies,
picturing her eating meat

rare at Vlados. Her voice is piped
through his headphones.
She says, 'Remain perfectly still,'
although nothing ever is.
Then *Something Blue* begins and he thinks,
'Almost nothing.'

His life repeats on the portable TV
                    power-drilled
to the hospital ceiling.
The actor playing him
is blonde but the Minobos
                    plays herself in
the sex scenes where
the he that is not *him*
presses the she that is *her*
                                        hard
                    into the bed — searching
for the part of her
that cannot lie.

The prisoners of the ward
        pull needles

                from arms,
        tubes from

                nasal cavities;
strike the linoleum floor

                hard

with the bare knuckles
of their purple faces.

A wasp is in the ward:

                    scrawling graffiti in negative

                    space:

tapping

against the windowpane:

               searching

      for the crack

that lets in

      the cold:

He dreams of Icarus
in a backless gown strapped
to a hospital cot
that is the bench seat of a Falcon
flying down a country two-lane
through a tunnel of ghost gums.
                    Overhead,
branches burnt phosphorescent
by high beams
smart bloodshot eyes.

The wasp
that was inside
                    the ward
is now inside
            (his head).

His head,
blunt as a bowling ball,
lies heavy
as the Somali nurse
polishes and rolls him
and the wasp
      strains to lift him
by his finger holes.
          Rises an erection instead.

His father leaves a message.
He is working his way south
with a metal detector and a kelpie,
trawling the scrub for *his* father —
the one planted on a day
white hot as a blizzard when,
shrinking in woollen suits,
the uncles and aunts circled their eldest
as he drew impatient crows to his shoulder.

      He has nothing to tell the old man
now that the gods in their spite
have struck him dumb — pressed
the base of his skull with their immoral thumb.
The world has tilted forever north —
he cannot help but fall that way.
There are no hands to hold him
      and so he falls.
There are no hands to raise him
        and so he crawls
to the red rust hills of Dookie — where
a goanna as long as the rust road is wide
climbs a widow-maker, stares him cold;
where, on the pub verandah, sits
old Frank's Da, rugged up in a recliner,
Lee Enfield raised to his shoulder.

And, so, he wakes,
        in strangeness, and claws
at the gurney in an ambulance
            racing north, siren singing,
as a wasp performs a pig Latin liturgy
on the tabernacle
      that is his tongue.

The owl floats across the darkened ward;
lands on the metal bed head
with a click. Stares, does not blink
at the face shining on the pillow,
white as a pharmaceutical moon.
Asks,

      'Did you fall?'
And the face replies,
'But first I flew.'
At which the owl nods,
'That much is true.
What falls must first fly.'
Shifts, claw to claw, then decides,
'But I have only ever flown.'
And blinks.

      And hops onto the pillow.
Baits her beak with his lazy eye.
And the face screams,
'Wait!

      How could you never fall?'
And the owl does not blink.

      Does not speak, but claws
her answer into his skin.

Wakes in a prison of his own making.
            Walks a maze of corridors
without doors. Turning right once,
twice, to infinity — measuring
with bare feet the polished cheek
of a floor forever cold —
not doubling back to where
a fluorescent sword fastened
to the light fixture trembles
from motor neurone degradation;
where, from the depths of
the bureaucracy of corridors, comes
the roar, carnivorous, childish,
of the one the priests abandoned
with the lie that the mythos
            would be its sanctuary
and not its cage

Claws
with bare hands
the bed —

a dead man
digging
his grave.

And on the third day
a seagull with ants for eyes
found him half-buried
in winter sand, wearing
a surgical gown and a hospital bracelet
on a stranger's wrist.
To keep her from feeding
in envy on his eyes
he threw the squalling wraith
Scrabble tiles,
offering the most expensive kind —
        Q, X, Z — but she,
knowing without vowels
there could be no music,
ate only those.

The art of becoming nothing
is redaction:

slicing away all sinew until
not a shadow can be found

reflected in the mirror —
not a word printed

on the page.

Old, yet always new,
desire not departing,
appetite redoubled, became
the blood and bone of him
         — unspoken/unseen — until
he was not a man but a grievance
to fly seven generations.
A paragraph of crows held their format,
wrote themselves across the unblinking sky—
mens rea scrolled round each leg
just above the claw.
Rewritten in an identical loop de loop,
terra firma rewound to
midnight last winter,
         when — wordless/wingless —
a dead man walked naked
the wrong way down the main street
of a town with a water tower
         but no traffic lights,
a courthouse hotel
         but no courthouse,
a police cell
         but no key,
as the first feather of a curse
practiced writing itself
         cursively — clockwise/anticlockwise—
in blood ink above.

Feathered souls blot out
          the sun:
a blood-ink eclipse.

The sky dreams
in dead languages:
scratches the corneas

of glass towers
with unrequited
          words.

The roses left
to die
in the backyard

rebel
with thorny
bloom.

The way the setting sun shadows
a stand of pines that had no right
to colonise the river bank,
but did and do and shall remain.
The way the silt island
                    surfaces at low tide.
The way children wade over:
paint each other black
with the silk of volcanoes
            that grind basalt to talcum in their sleep.

He laps the oval while,
in the distance,
metronome skyscrapers
keep time;
chases the black dog
that chased him around
Hyde Park that winter;
collects dog turds in
recycled shopping bags,
wears a trace in the grass
that becomes a tail
he must catch as the dogs,
congregating on the concrete wicket
at the apex of the oval,
track his shadow
to tell their time.

The wasps in the umbrella tree,
exclamation marks
in search of an ending.
Turn people into verbs.
Paw at the evening.
Jerk upright as though marionettes,
dancing one two three once more,
at the school ball
where boys wear shirts untucked
and girls the best dresses
        their mothers could afford.
Where another storm kicks
the ceiling of the basketball stadium
as though it were the stubborn key
on a typewriter. Such is
the monotony of punctuation.
Because when it rains
        it rains.
Because when it is dry
        it is dry.
Because the run on sentence
of the horizon
        is a page
that can only be turned.

Doors painted red,
summer night drowsy with smoke,
he walks out to the courtyard.
Says, 'Firewords,'
                    instead of fireworks.
Apologises to Caligula,
the crossbred canine.
'My mind's not right, Cal.'
The Japanese willow,
also middle-aged, has thickened
where he has thinned, scratches
his head with a sympathetic branch.
'Much obliged,' he says,
'*Gong Xi Fa Cai.*'
Apologises again.
'You don't speak Mandarin, do you?'
And the willow offers
not a whisper in reply,
'Neither do I.'
                    More firewords.
Somewhere, somewhere close,
people are talking in a backyard.
A barbecue is burning flesh.
Cal brushes against him and
he leans hard against the willow,
where a mosquito finds him,
                    gives him an *ang pow* kiss
to mark the going and the coming
of the year of the wasp.

'Click on the headlights,'
he says, as their wagon descends
a blue-black carpet of bitumen
into the one-way tunnel
to the underworld.
                    'Everything
is luminous,' he says, 'everything
is white.
The fog too thick, too thin, and I
too tired to fight.'
                    And she says,
'There is no fog,
there is no sun.
The way is clear and the lights burn
for us;
beckon us to come.'

And the man asked the mountain,

'How does it feel to become
something more than desire?'

And the mountain asked the man,

'Something less,
you mean?

It would feel as though

the sun stared too hard,
the sky forgot to rain,

the rivers lost their way.'

Drowning in darkness,
car buffeted on the bluff,
they wait
for the Ferris wheel of the horizon
to crawl forwards
and face another day of fire.

And call this faith.

EIGHT VIEWS OF NOWHERE

Contemplate her eight views of nowhere:
            these eight views of myself
to which she made me an accessory.
Gaze unblinking into the mirrored,
reversed world of an extinction in progress,
a transfiguration from infinity to infirmary,
            delusion to allusion, god to wasp.
And the wasps, born anew
                        diurnally as deities would,
should they be reproduced to scale on
the digital archival paper that holds these views,
            be reborn as dragons
                        to rival Ishiro Honda's keiju —
ink jet manifestations of the past anxieties
            of our tokusetsu life. As for today,
fear sets me free, gives me flight,
                        transforms me from an insect
into something greater/lesser, blinding me
to the moment fast approaching when
            these wings are no longer able to defy
gravity and I, too, shall fall
                        from the monochrome sky
and break my imagined self against
            the footpath of a confected world.
Still, there is truth in this chicanery.
Truth, that the satellite image of
a Pacific atoll is a sham

made luminescent not by Fukushima
but by the residual of a water stain
left on a studio floor in East Kew;
that the mountains are made
            of self-raising flour,
that the drowned cities are stacked
containers of plastic, that the moon rising
is the parabolic arc of the heat shield
of a saucepan seen in cross-section,
that everything
            is as it should be,
that nothing — nowhere — is as it seems.

I am keiju's model.
An approximation of an imagination
that causes B-grade movie extras to scream
            and run for the all-too-short
remaining moments
                        of their nameless lives.
I am everywhere —
                        omnipotent at my cruising altitude,
all seeing with my dorsal ocelli —
as high sierras of self-raising flour,
            half-obscured in the mist,
stretch forever from right to left across
            paper scrolls that appear
oceanic, almost pacific.

Is familiar.

      Is strange.

Is the forgotten
landscape of forgetting.
Is the definition of *nowhere*.

      A place where somewhere
loses its name, where

            someone loses their way.
And the sky is
a sky of the coldest cobalt-blue.

      And the great white cloud is
sleeping on the ground.
And the face of the ocean,

      devoid of oxygen,
is black as tar.

Night rain sweeps
from the west,
wearing a slip
of silken smoke
to mask memories.

Stings and does not slake.

I stared at the origami vaginas
                              until
            the heat of my gaze
caused
            the edges of each to fringe
and curl,
                        unwrap fold by fold:
dissolve
            into an eternity of white.

If this star of my affection
were love enough
                  no darkness would you see,
but shadows of a longing.
             The negative of an ardour,
hard as obsidian,
that will burn until I fade —
             blind the eternity of midnights
with the blink of one midday.

TIME'S CARRION COMPASS COURSE

Following the many elbows of the Yarra.

Taking the racing line.

Retracing the route to the Toorak school that
did not teach, but bequeathed a tie.
Perhaps, I was blinded
by the nostalgia of a life half lived,
perhaps, and did not see
the vixen spirit herself across the road
just in time to feel the bite of my tyres.
There was no time to brake.
My foot was half on,

half off, the accelerator
when I felt the shock of her through
my steering wheel, heard her cry.
I could have kept driving into the night —
the road was dead, the streets asleep —
but could not forget that time when,
coming down Brown Mountain in a Toyota,
I killed a goanna and kept going,

lacked the decency
to drag her carcass off the road,
and how I carried that sin
in my glove compartment still.
I stopped. Stepped out into the early morning,
the air cold enough to turn breath to steam,
and stood by the taillights of my old 318,
watched the fox lie in the glare of a street light,
half a world away from her natural home,

and felt something close to pity.

Waited until a fleeting shadow
— at first an eclipse —
grew smaller, darker, then manifested
as a wedge-tailed eagle that landed
on the double-white line without a sound,
wing tips sweeping the leaves
from the blue-black road.
The eagle was telling me
she was watching me
watch the fox.
So, now I knew I had no choice.
I had to act. I left my car behind,
purring its soft red cloud of carcinogens,
and heard my boots strike the bitumen
as I drew close enough to see my animus
reflected in her animal eye.
The vixen was breathing
— more like panting —
and unable to move more than her head.
Without thinking, I reached down
to touch her burnt orange fur,
but she had seen enough of my kind
on her backyard travels
and, throwing her head up, caught
my thumb in the trap of her razor teeth.
What happened next surprised us all.
Without speaking,
I took off my old school tie
to bind my bleeding hand,

walked back to the car,
          popped the boot and came
back to the fox with the wheel jack
swinging low from my good hand,
then let that hand rise and fall
beneath the shadow of the street light,
and listened to the sound
          of steel splintering bone
while the eagle lifted herself from the road
to seek solace in the sky.

A whirlpool of sparrows
perform a perfect *om*,
                        but the circle
            is too perfect.
They are not birds,
but a scree of drones
                triangulating
the what —
            if not
                        the why —
of life ever ending.
                Aggregating infinities.
Keeping score.

she is

     my warmth
         my intermission
     my naked midday
     my conjugation

is she

Face a fist,
seven years of muscle
rising eight,
she forces me to lean hard
          to hold her flat
on the table
as the doctor — who
insists on being called Daisy —
          dabs liquid nitrogen
into my daughter's sole.

I hear cold skin burning
as I tell her to be brave,
          but the truth is
she is brave enough already.

It takes courage to be scared.

I woke on a beach
of hard white pills

with the moronic tide licking
my weaker hand.

The one that tremors
at its fingertips,

causing me to break
what once I fixed.

I scrunched pharmaceuticals
between my toes,

lifted the ocean to my mouth
and swallowed.

The waves will come again
tomorrow.

Carnivore crows fly
east by west by
south by north to feast
on the banquet of our duty —
　　　　mark time's carrion compass course.
And it is a mystery to me
why the killers are heralded
while the faceless dead
are said to blame.
　　　　And, I must confess,
it is not just the sin that sickens,
but its plagiarism.
O country that is —
　　　　that is not — my country,
that follows me home
like some mongrel on a dirt road
that traces the spine of a broken levee
as backyard dogs goad themselves
into a frenzy, know this:
　　　　I would rather shoot you for a stray
than follow your path another day.

This devil's bridge
buttressed by the bleached stones
of bodies broken

          by our scourge.
This narrow relief
from the maw of eternity
around which the fretful track winds

       up into the marbled clouds
that promised rain, then

      broke.
These flagstones hewn
from the petrified faces of
those turned back,

      those drowned,
those embalmed alive

         with razor wire.
The unblinking accusation of

      the forever unclosed eyes
of those forever children
that burn the soles
of marching feet.
This nation we made ours.
Ours alone.

The auguries of the wasp
were not in its flight
       but the sting
that made me crush
its winged trigonometry
with the weight of my offended heel.
       To kill the messenger,
they say, is a sin that seals
the fate of the recipient,
darkening time's equation,
       stilling air so that
her face loses all mystery,
is no longer innocent; while,
in some crowded hive,
a riot is awakened — for
every killing demands a reply,
       a reckoning — and so
the countless siblings stir themselves
into an ecstasy, a welcome change
from the certainty of a winter dawn
as nameless millions begin to hum and swarm.

Let us talk of Knoxville, Tennessee,
and summer nights lying sweet and
low in the long grass listening
to the softwood trees read James Agee.
Let us talk about talking about the futility of fences
and barefoot children and parents unbuttoned
to belts that no longer feel the need to
whip clean dirty brown legs.
Let us jump up and bless ourselves
with the sprinkler
and coil the hose tight.
Let us lie down and think
but not speak (not one word)
about the glow on the horizon
we took to be the sun rising
but was instead Tokyo burning.
Let us and our children and our children's children
not be burned to the bone.
Let us talk about the sorrow of being.
Let us waterboard General LeMay until he explains
how a killer is a hero is a father is a son.
Let us pilot a drone in Afghanistan from
a penny arcade in Anaheim.
Let us ride *Magic Mountain* until the trees
run out of leaves. Let us fly
under five thousand feet so
they can feel our engines humming,
hear the whiz of each and every M-69.

Let us explain that what we did was not Guernica
nor Bergen-Belsen nor Dresden,
was not war nor terror nor crime
                    — just slaughter. Let us argue
at the Hague that the prisoners of Manus Island
are not people but haunted boku-zukin —
and that what is hidden beneath those hoods
is no longer human. Let us believe
that a quilted kimono with a cotton mask is
protection against the firestorm that is to come
                    when the cities of the world fall
through the floor of the world.
Let us give thanks for that which we shall receive
when they who shall be slaughtered in our name
are led into that abattoir of good intentions.
Let us walk empty streets with the stars
for judgment and, through steaming breath,
                    quote Heinrich Heine and recite
Slaughter House Five verbatim.
Let us crash land our Bikko —
that great shining silverfish of a Superfortress —
in the black waters off Manhattan and know
that Reznikoff was right. Let us admit that,
yes, that was chaos through which we stumbled,
that is chaos we cast our eyes back upon
and chaos it is that shall forever remain.

What makes the heart grow?
It is not absence —
          no —
but the penumbra of your presence.
That is not to say our love is without flaw —
          those days when your anger lingers
in the bedroom like cordite;
          those nights when the acid of my soul
spills out of me, burns through the gristle,
bone and skin of me; scorches the carpet.
Which is how it should be, I suppose,
because life is combat and love
a fortress from the fray —
and the stones of our tower,
cut by hand, are not square,
          but —
mirroring the undulations of your
          beauty —
pleasing to my eye.
And the fires within these walls
will not sleep
until we can no longer wake.
I would like to say otherwise,
say that such a day shall never come;
that our time will be unending,
our fires an eternity of sunsets
as luminous and unyielding as napalm —
          but I cannot.

There are no happy endings.
There is no life eternal.
There is only grace ephemeral.
Remember Box Hill Hospital?
How the doctor showed,
      in real time,
the ultrasound of my beating heart,
pointed out the tendril scar wrapped
ghostly around each grey-scale chamber.
'Tracing the betrayal,' she said.
'A time when the involuntary muscle
almost failed to meet its duty.'
And as she spoke I relived —
      I did —
the years and months, days and hours,
of that great unhappiness that never
      turned —
thickening the blood until it seized.
My heart was that frail;
that feckless.
And that is why I will not beg the Fates
      for mercy,
for one day more than is my due.
As for the gods —
      who knows? —
perhaps they now reside in open-source software
rather than our hearts,
which are full enough for now.

And, so, I pray to the digital celestials
to program me this day,
my daily bread, and —

      should tomorrow come —
to give me the love I have loved
all my adult days
so that I might watch her clockwise
shadow
track the diurnal passage of the chariot
of the sun.
And that will have to be enough —

      it will —

for, though we have no time to live,
we have just enough time to love.

Acknowledgements

I would like to thank my publisher John Hunter for his continued support; Lisa Gorton, Alisa Dodge, Robert Minhinnick, and Paul Mitchell for their poetic advice; Dan Disney for prodding me in an unexpected poetic direction; Meredith Squires and William Kelly for their artistic inspiration; the coordinator of Passionate Tongues Poetry, Michael Reynolds, for giving me a stage on which I could test drive early versions of several poems in this collection; and my wife, Kirsten, for saving me.

The vast majority of these poems have not been published before, reflecting my reluctance to part with poems while in the midst of a poetic cycle. Thanks to Bronwyn Lea for getting me started on this manuscript by prompting me to publish a poem in the *Australian Poetry Journal*. Thanks to *Australian Book Review*, *Verity La,* and *Meanjin* for publishing poems at the end of the cycle.

NOVELTIES
FIONA HILE

Winner of the Kenneth Slessor Prize, 2014

'Unique, subtle, exuberant and smart, Fiona Hile's poetry is transformative, a sudden arrest in all the imagination can bear.'
— Peter Minter

'Novelties *is absolutely singular poetry … It opens holes in knowledge and subtracts truths … Poets, beware: a figure like Milton or Lucretius walks here among us!*'
—AJ Carruthers, *Cordite*

In her first full-length collection, Fiona Hile applies the ambitions and strategies of fiction to produce genuinely novel poems that signal 'a state of poetic emergency'.

Novelties resonates with themes of nature, love, and literature, showcasing Hile's command of style and form to reveal an assertive and intriguing new voice.

DEVIOUS INTIMACY
ANN VICKERY

'These poems cut right through cultural habit and cant
and put paid to any "theoried regrets". This is arrestingly
incarnated poetry diffused with female luminosity.'
— Pam Brown

Devious Intimacy combines a sly, playful wit with a
melancholic tenderness to navigate between the
private world of love and sexuality and wider forms of
connection, teasing out how past histories and literature
underscore contemporary human bonds.

From Abstract Expressionism to Test Cricket, Vickery's
poetry delves into that which delights and intrigues us,
both celebrating and critiquing our everyday routines
and aesthetic modes of reception. Wry, smart, and
bristling with acute observation, Devious Intimacy is a
beguiling mix of charm and charge.

NOT FOX NOR AXE
CHLOE WILSON

'Chloe Wilson is among the most promising of Australia's younger poets … *Not Fox Nor Axe* is a stunning mixture of myth, history and natural history, demonstrating both her ability to find new and intriguing angles on her subjects and her wit and dexterity with language.'— Ron Pretty

Women knit at the foot of the guillotine. Hundreds of blackbirds tumble suddenly from the sky. Red Riding Hood's grandmother speaks from the belly of the wolf. Santa Lucia offers you her eyes on a platter.

These poems present a panorama, by turns historical, mythical, and modern, of horrors and absurdities both familiar and obscure. 'Perhaps not fox nor axe, but something gives us chase' – and the only thing more difficult than bearing witness is turning away.

SMALL TOWN SOUNDTRACK
BRENDAN RYAN

'*In a tradition that includes Les Murray and Philip Hodgins, Ryan reminds us of the harshness of much country life … His poetry, with its unflinching portrayal of dairy farming and associated small-town life, is surely essential reading for inner-city cafe habitués.*'
— Geoff Page, *The Australian*

Small Town Soundtrack continues Brendan Ryan's exploration of place and belonging that resonate in country towns.

From the lives of farmers and abattoir workers to the history of aboriginal dispossession. From a tour of the communities of the Mt Noorat Football League in Victoria's isolated Western District to moments of wonder on back country roads.

Lyrical and rich in narrative power *Small Town Soundtrack* dismantles the idealized rural pastoral with an empathetic and incisive voice.

THE MUNDIAD
JUSTIN CLEMENS

Shortlisted for the Kenneth Slessor Prize, 2014

'*The Mundiad* is an antidote to the poetry of sensibility. It's a roiling, bilious reminder of how good poetry can be when its propelled by an angry dismay at the world's myriad inadequacies.' — Dr Chris McAuliffe

'A fabulously irreverent rant … Scholarly without being ponderous, beautifully elegiac about popular culture and witty to boot.' — Pam Brown

Modelled on classical epics such as Virgil's *Aeneid* and Pope's *Dunciad*, *The Mundiad* is a blistering satire of the contemporary world — a world of deranged superstars, climate-change deniers, rogue states, multimedia extravaganzas, political bullshit, creepy talkback demagogues, financial crises, child soldiers, happy idiots, genetic engineering, death camps, pornographers and more.

CONTENT
LIAM FERNEY

'Ferney's poems gun their way through a globalised economy with acronyms, diminutives, and inventive linguistic flares that light up the personal as it intertwines with, and often rams like a dodgem car against, the 24/7 history-making machinations of power. *Content* lampoons and laments the narcissism that accompanies the supposed information age in which "We have traded greatness for convenience".'
— Gig Ryan

Content uses the argot of politics and the internet to tackle religion, war, love and late capitalism.

This is fast paced poetry that is critically engaged and explosive--a hand grenade tossed into the middle of polite society.